Cowries & Spiked Tea

(A Collection of Poems and Raw Thoughts)

Cowries & Spiked Tea

(A Collection of Poems and Raw Thoughts)

Essmorra

Printed in the United States of America

First Printing, 2023

ISBN: 978-1-962446-05-1

YOUR STORY MATTERS

The Butterfly Typeface Publishing
PO Box 56193
Little Rock AR 72215

www.thebutterflytypeface.com

Dedication

This book is dedicated to the fire in you; the time is now to sow the seeds that will produce your dream.

"I have a duty to speak the truth as I see it and share not just my triumphs, not just the things that felt good, but the pain. The intense, often unmitigated pain. It is important to share how I know survival is survival and not just a walk through the rain."
Audre Lorde

Table of Contents

Mood Setter

Light your candles or incense.
Download my COWRIES AND SPIKED TEA PLAYLIST
ON APPLE MUSIC AND SPOTIFY, fix yourself a nice drink,
and for my non-drinkers, fix an elixir of choice.
Kick ya feet up and enjoy the ride.

Essmorra

Apple Kool-Aid

- 1 ¼ oz Crown Royal Apple Whiskey
- 1oz cran-apple juice
- With a few cubes of ice and an apple wedge

Wine Selections

- Chilled Riesling
- Chilled Pinot Grigio

Acknowledgments

Life and all of my earthly lessons; I'm thankful for the journey and healing along the way, shout out to my spiritual team of family and friends for having my back every step of the way.

I'd like to thank all the supporters that I've gained over time; words really can't express the gratitude in my heart.

Tran'e Gilliam, I'm so grateful for your friendship. You've been on this writing journey for a while now. Thank you for your extra set of eyes. I love you to pieces.

Kiana Monae, thank you for continuing to capture my vision and bringing them to life through your artwork. You are truly a gem.

Jade Denton (CULTR PWR CEO), I'm proud of our growth and thankful for your transparency. Thank you for assisting me with the visual art for this project. Love you always!

Definitions:

Cowries:
shells that symbolize divine feminine beauty, luck, and wealth.

Spiked Tea:
an elixir of choice that encourages me to Talk My Shyt

Apple Kool-Aid

That's what he called his whiskey or beer.

Maybe because he didn't want me to know

that's how he buried trauma.

Prescott is a dry county.

So, rides to the country to get a case

and 5th from the bootlegger,

for a sip of that liquid,

to forget the PTSD cards that life dealt.

And a prayer hoping that he makes it upstairs.

"I heard your prayer, Pawpa,"

as I pour out libations for you.

Rest In Peace, because the world didn't deserve you.

She tore you into pieces and apple kool-aid

kept you glued together, so you can keep your kool.

RIP JERRY and MIDNIGHT

First of My Name

Essmorra.

First and last of my name.

I am the original.

Master of all my pieces.

Queen. Pioneer. Poetic priestess.

MUVA

As I stretch out

I can't help but think

about this majestic moment

that we manifested with true Black love.

I'm a Life-giver,

portal,

muva,

umi,

hooyo.

And best of all

Prince Mdjai's mommy.

Excited about our new addition

to our kingdom.

Excited to see our creation.

Excited to glow and grow in love with you

more each day.

We're ready for your

grand entrance.

Ready to love you past the

many moons and stars.

The universe has concocted

Black love and

look at what we started.

For Idella Khalifah

PURGE

Purging poems

from

my soul.

Opening up.

Letting it go!

Some shit new, some shit old.

As long as it doesn't have a hold

on my growth.

Facing my truth to keep it real,

so that my mind can finally be still.

So I'm purging poems out of me

so that I'm able to dance.

So that I am free.

Who I do it Fo

I don't do this for me.

I do it for the ancestors,

that paved many ways for me.

I do this with the power that was vested in me.

I do this to be a voice for every sister and every brother.

and every person that's been classified as a color.

The ones that had to mark *other*.

Labeled in America's system that dismisses them,

wanting us to fall in place.

Marching to robotic rhythms.

Trying to rid us of our souls,

with fucked up curriculums.

And schemes engineered for the betterment of mankind

that ain't really that kind.

The kind we're out here.

Dying spiritually and mentally.

Catching strays.

Bullets, that is.

Liquid brains from learning the same old shit.

They say insanity is repeating things

and expecting change.

They say insanity is repeating things

and expecting change!

So, why do we keep going round

in the barrel of merrys revolver?

Following America's old laws,

like they're solutions to our problems.

We can't change without change.

And change is something we need more than ever.

I feel like I'm an old-school record.

On repeat because of how many times

have we heard that.

"I'm speaking for the ones before me."

Pac said it best, if there's no hope for the youth.

Then it's no hope for the future!"

DAMN...

"If there's no hope for the youth,

then, it's no hope for the future!"

A mess

I'm stressed,

I know that I'm a mess!

But in a world full of she(s),

there's only one me!

Which is a blessing just like these lessons

that I catch on a daily.

Overthinking all

the maybes,

the hows,

and only if

I didn't overthink things,

because things happen …

Everything is as it should be.

You deserve me and I you.

We can do this love thing.

I'm cool if, you're cool.

Studying me like I'm school,

but, breaking all the rules to society's

1, 2, and 3rd step (rules); we make our own!

We're grown!

See, I imagine you strumming my body

like you do your guitar.

Loving on me and setting me free,

but, I'm a mess

because I'm afraid of the one thing I want most.

That's L.O.V.E!

Too Much

Aye!

You know what?

Maybe, I am too much.

Too much bronze skin.

Too much thick lips.

Too much thick hips with the juicy tits.

Too much fro.

Too much glow.

And Negro, since I'm just that much, you can go!

Over here trying to stunt my growth!

H.O.E.
(Happiness Ova Everythang)

I feel good!

So good,

better than ever.

More than I ever

Believed I could.

Better than I thought I deserved.

Treating myself like I should have always been.

I shaved off my insecurities and impurities

that had me thinking,

"No, you can't,"

"No, you shouldn't,"

"Why would you?"

I know now that I'm capable of whatever

I want in my sanctuary.

My universe.

My world!

It feels good to put myself 1st.

Finally!

Feels good to finally feel freedom.

Freedom between my toes.

Freedom in my hair.

Freedom in what I write.

Damn, I'm just happy to feel good!

I'm happy about every inch of freedom that I obtain,

On my journey of my womanhood.

Imagination

Imagination is connecting us

somewhere

that's just not here ...

Imagine That

Imagine me sitting on your lap, facing forward,

while I run my fingers across your head.

While you're tonguing down my breast

and sucking on my nipples,

the wetness of your tongue turns me on.

Each stroke from your full tongue wettens my poonany.

She pulsates for you.

Do you feel the heartbeat?

She beats for you.

She beats for the extraordinary adventure.

Your thick,

Black,

strong

dick is gonna take her on.

She beats for the love you give her.

She tightens and showers you in appreciation.

She grips you to show you love back.

Together we moan a song in your name.

While you're beating down my drums

filled with our rhythm,

I imagine the pleasure will last forever.

Ruby Woo

Red paint, thick lips.

Sometimes, I tell lies to distract you

from whatever truth lies in my eyes.

Devil's Food

Platonic rendezvous

Has my stomach in knots.

Every time you come through,

or whenever I think about you.

Chocolate on chocolate,

like devils food,

dark and sweet.

You handle me with care,

treating me like a delicate flower

because you know I'm unique.

You speak life into me and I you.

I watch us grow every day.

I can't get enough of the fire

that you set in my chest.

You make everything I thought was fake.

Feel Real.

You're the truth.

Is it safe to say you're my boo?

I don't wanna walk on eggshells anymore.

I'm willing to go all the way with you!

Sunrise

You brighten the day when you're here.

And when you're gone, it's like the sun was never here.

I need you.

Or, at least, I feel like I do.

I like when you get a rise out of me

because I get a rise out of you.

Turquoise Blue Liquid Love

Turquoise

Blue liquid love

flowing on this hot summer day.

I scramble all of my thoughts

to make sure that I have the right things to say,

to make you notice me.

Careful not to overdo it

because I'd be embarrassed if I blew it.

Turquoise

Blue liquid love

brewing in my pot.

Butterflies stirring up the emotions in my ribs

that cage my guts to say what I have to say.

What I need to say

Is trapped.

My mouth is muted.

Every time you pass me by

I'm scared that I'll scare you away

With all that I want to give ...

All that I want to have with you.

I've been smothering my mind

with all the what if's

and the gift of the time that we spend.

What if we ...

intoxicated each other with what we deserve?

Real love!

Those good hugs!

Booty rubs!

Creating Black-on-Black love!

Proving to ourselves that it's still very real

and we don't have to hide how we feel.

We don't need anyone's permission

to share kisses.

You know those passionate ones

that make it feel like a thousand suns

are hitting your body?

Not sure if you're tingling from love darts

or melting like a summer rocky road ice cream cone.

But love magic got us gone.

Love has embedded herself deep within us!

Chances

Life is supposedly full of games

and I don't play with toys.

I decided to take a chance anyway

and rolled the dice.

Thank God you aren't a lil ass boy!

Walked away from my X,

I took a turn for the best.

360.

When we part ways,

I know you miss me

and I, slick, miss you too.

I don't tell you,

but, you know you my boo.

I'm strategic about my next move

to protect what's in my *ches'*.

Nah,

I'm not used to this.

But, I know this right here ain't no mess!

When you're around I'm assured

from your authenticity

that you're true to this.

The ride I'm on,

you're not really new to this.

And You're here for

next-level type shit.

Tea & incense

Fire on high, the room is filled with warmth.

All four corners of this space are exhaling sage,

with a touch of his scent

that's still lingering on me.

I can still taste

the warm herbal elixirs with honey lemon drops

on my tongue.

from when we made each other cum.

He and I

danced all night long,

savoring each other's

passion fruit.

Tea and incense make me wild for you!

LOCK BOX

Your dick is the key to my lock.

You unleashed

my floodwaters.

Breaking boundaries,

revealing secrets

foreign to my body.

And it's hard for me to move on to another body

because I know it's only one key

that connects me to that euphoric place.

And you plus me is the magic combination

that leads us to orgasmic constellations.

Our bodies dance while

having orgasmic conversations.

Our moans

are our music.

I wish I could leave our song on repeat.

I get chills all over my body

thinking about those excursions.

Mmmm, how revolutionary of us to

love on each other freely.

Sex on each other freely.

To exist freely in front of each other

while being unapologetic.

Mother earth's children of the wild.

connecting like the fiery stars in the sky.

Our story was already written

when I first hugged you.

Our story was already written

when I first kissed you.

Our story was already written

when you unlocked my box ...

Magic Stick

I asked him what he was doing.

He told me he just got into bed.

My reply was, "I'm about to hop in mine, too.

I should be over there with you."

Getting butt rubs

and licking on them tattoos.

We talking shit about

that new shit we gone do.

I'ma ride it fast and later

we *gonna* chop and screw

each other's brains out.

Round after round somebody gonna

tap out.

Hard wood and a soft ass.

Somebody *gonna* be screaming my name out

or calling on God.

Two freaks tangled in

sheets.

I *wanna* suck your majestical

wood,

Until your juicy blessings

drip down my lips

and I swallow love.

When you enter me,

I'll gush like a geyser

and we'll elevate

to ecstasy.

Him

Cheekbones higher than the midnight sky

in the month of July.

His rich, chocolate complexion

warms me.

All the hairs on my body are no longer laying down.

He has my undivided attention.

When I gaze into

his eyes, they tell his truth.

A story I can't seem to get enough of.

Divine Black man,

with your intelligent ass

stimulating me with more lessons

than the schoolhouse has ever had.

Because you've

walked it.

Lived it.

And breathed it.

You be it.

I'm intrigued

by your GODfidence.

Walking round here

owning this shit.

Certain with yourself, can't nobody disorientate you.

You know where you stand!

Trust

Trust.

Why do we give it to people who don't deserve it?

Why do we give people the benefit of the doubt?

Truth

It's the truth.

Careful, the truth can be deep.

So, it's what I speak

because I want it to seep down into your soul.

I want it to make you think.

I want it to leak like a serum

into your bloodstream.

Truth.

Can you handle the depths that it'll reach?

Can you handle what it'll make surface?

Truth.

Can you face it?

Can you swallow it whole?

Can you take it?

It's levels to this shit.

It's beautiful and ugly at the same damn time.

The Clock

Time told

how long it would take

for you to fold.

I wasn't supposed to cry

but I shed a few tears anyway.

Couple of months

and a few days,

I counted

when you stopped being consistent.

You acted as if my presence was non-existent.

Missed calls.

Ignored texts.

My intuition

lead me to your secrets,

the ones to be kept between you and her.

Don't fret she didn't tell.

You can't look me in my face

with steady eyes.

You're full of lies.

Tiptoeing around like I can't tell.

Wonder how long

you'll go

thinking I don't know?

You reek of her spirit.

Time told,

you folded.

You ain't even know it!

Get Out My Kitchen

Stop begging for a seat at my dinner table,

when you can't handle the heat from my kitchen.

It's understood why you keep

bothering me,

because you know what you been missing.

I don't keep leftovers.

And

Nigga

No,

you can't come over!

1-800– His-Loss

He texted me to tell me he missed me.

I stared at the message and smirked.

I thought about all the affection

that I put in.

I thought about all of the time

that I put in.

The countless missed calls and text messages with no
replies.

Lies…

That kept me with wet eyes

and smeared mascara.

The tears made me tougher!

The tears made me wiser!

The tears I won't let fall anymore!

I refuse to release them

because you've been missing them, too.

Right along with all the good shit I brought forth

to you.

Who knew it would have taken this long

to really be through

with you?

He texted me to tell me he missed me.

I stared at the message.

Replied,

"Who's this?"

With a grin,

I said,

"You must have the wrong number."

I sent another text that read,

"1-800-447-5677"

(1-800– HIS-LOSS)

Don't Save 'Em

I resurrected my pen to talk about my deadly sins.

The treason I've committed against myself.

Violation after violation.

Boundaries, what are those?

Selling myself dreams of what someone else can be,

after I've been shown

my placement in their lives.

I still swoop down like a hawk for its prey,

or a bitch with a cape,

trying to save the day.

Until I realized,

I am not

a band-aid,

and my pussy ain't no benevolence offering.

Pitty-Pat With My Soul

I still smell your cologne on my pillows.

I still taste your tongue on my tongue

while our legs were intertwined.

Old connections

and our

flawed perfections.

That tie us close but, we're still so far apart,

playing pitty-pat with each other's hearts.

Our souls singing familiar songs,

reminding us that we haven't outgrown each other.

Reminding us that we aren't done

with each other.

Reminding us that we'll always be lovers.

Our time

is always short,

and I hate it because time hasn't run out on us

or what we have.

And neither one of us can explain it.

But, this bond has become threaded into our DNA

and I don't know how to undo it

and makes me wonder if somehow,

this is all God's doings.

Am I being punished?

Is it karma from the past?

I'm being starved from the only love that I yearn to have.

I want that from him.

No one else

Can make my heart beat like an ancestral drum,

while I cum and erupt love on top of love.

Not sure where it's coming from,

but you pull it out of me.

See, I hold on to things you've done for me

and to the things you've said to me.

I hold on to how you made me feel.

Dreaming that one day

We can make it our reality.

But,

It's like I'm fighting against gravity.

I know that our encounters are temporary

and your sun will orbit around my moon,

and align ourselves for a short period of time.

An eclipse made from love

that's been cultivated from the unknown.

Random

So threaded into my DNA,

your name pops in my head at least once a day,

and your face in my imagination all the time.

It's like I almost belong to you or something,

but we both know that I don't.

The Question

"To be

or

not to be?"

Was never the question.

Because to be:

is to exist

without question.

And everyday

millions of questions come rushing

to my head.

Staring at myself in the mirror

trying to figure out,

who

or

what

I want to be,

when I can be,

when I should be,

and how to be who I think I am,

when sometimes I be nobody.

I mean, I be a body

that's going with the flow,

riding with the currents,

trying to stay aboard my own ship,

avoiding

debris that's surrounding me.

Trying not to flip my shit.

So, I pray to myself for myself,

asking Goddesses to cover me.

Help me

figure out who I be.

Help me see me because right now I cannot see

who me is,

who I be.

All I know is that I'm here right now

and I don't know what for.

To be or not to be?

To be

or not to be?

What kind of question is that?

You asked me that the first time,

you see I didn't respond back.

To be is to exist without question.

Mind Pollution

Right now, things are a little shitty.

Yet and still,

I hold my head high

because I'm pretty

on the outside.

But, I'm pretty damn broken on the inside,

with hopes that I too will rise like Maya,

into thin air.

It's hard walking around like this shit don't hurt.

I'm mad that I care,

when the world don't!

My mind won't give me a break and I'm

not sure how much of this I can take.

Trying to break generational cycles,

but the cyclones are so fast I get sucked back in.

Getting tested by men

who are willing to lay but leave again.

Like my great grandma

and mama and *nem* said,

"All these he's,

him's,

and misters

stuck on the pleasures of whatever

they fantasize

I can do to their dick."

Looking Glass

Saw you today …

For the first time, it was more than a reflection,

more than potential,

more than anything I'd thought I'd be.

But, for the first time, I have seen me

in my raw form born to perform and speak these words

that have never been heard.

This looking glass was like no other.

The reflection I saw was confidence that had been

confidential for so long.

Now a cocoon birthing a butterfly,

who's weathered many storms…

Storms that have now passed and are

things far in my past thanking the most high

for a new light.

A new path.

This new pass to be "Me" unapologetically

manifesting light and all these glorious things unto me.

Because I deserve to fall in love with this girl

turned woman in the looking glass,

no longer mad at her past

But, rejoicing because I'm overcoming censorship,

fear, failure, and anything I heard that I couldn't be.

I'm free because I am me!

This looking glass

has always shown me who I was.

I'm no longer afraid of who I see in the looking glass!

In my head

Wanted to spend more time

to ease our minds from

earthly stressors,

a lesson,

a blessing.

Your name is the first familiar thing to my thoughts.

Picked up the phone to dial your number,

but pride is failing me.

I don't *wanna* look like a fool again.

So, I blame it on muscle memory.

Sometimes I wish I stayed blind

just to get back that peace,

a hit,

one last time.

FU

I'm not the bitch to get you ready

for the bitch you wanna be with.

Mufucka, I'm supreme.

I'm a dream girl's dream.

And I don't have time to hope and pray

that you act right.

I don't have time for inconsistent

walks down your fake ass straight and narrow.

I don't have time for your narcissism.

I severed ties with the lies.

You used to cut me with Sharp, "I love yous"

that turned to "fuck yous."

So fuck you!

So

fuck

you!

Shut Off Notice

Been trying to heal my self-inflicted wounds

because it's way past due.

Got so many notices that I was supposed to

have been pass you.

Should have been left you,

but I was busy trying to make do with what you gave.

Scrapping what's left of us back together,

thinking that I could save you from your traumas

nurse you back to health like I was your mama.

Taking on unnecessary stress

and drama;

I did it to show you that I could handle a test.

I did it to show you I was better than the rest.

Not realizing that I was committed to someone

who was ok with me committing spiritual suicide,

helping with my jaded views on love.

Lately, I've been thanking goddess

for this new-found darkness.

Now, that the lights are back on,

I lost you,

and I'm trying to be ok with not finding you ...

this time.

BAND-AID

My vagina isn't a band-aid

to heal your emotional traumas.

I don't deserve no drama from you or your baby mama.

Boy Bye

I'm not *yo* cum rag,

just *cuz* you *wanna* cum bad.

Fucking on you is fun from the past.

Grace

How amazing it would be

if I blessed you one more time

with my forgiveness,

with my presence,

my unconditional love.

Grace.

It's what you expect me to give

every single time you

fuck up,

fuck me over,

and expect us to start over.

Grace.

I've given so long

yo ass think that shit is free.

Now, there is a cost.

I'm done letting you cross boundaries for free.

You have to pay the consequences

for all the

disrespect and pain you've caused me.

The right thing for me to do is return the favor,

but I'll decline my fleshes' desire to fuck you up.

I'll give myself some grace this time

and watch you suffer from my silence.

Seasonal Allergies

You were a season.

That's the reason our love wouldn't and couldn't grow.

And there I was, acting like I didn't know.

Masking how I felt so that you'd still be here with me,

to make me feel like I was enough.

Even though your head was gone,

your heart was hers.

And your dick was mine, from time to time.

It kept me hanging on to the blurred lines

of a love contract that had been technically

null and void for years.

I was scared to sever the ties

because I thought you were the only someone

who could love me,

because I only loved you.

I was loyal to you.

No matter what you did,

I let you invade me.

After you played me,

I felt it in my gut every time.

And every time it knocked breath out of me.

Yet and still, I wanted to be blind.

I believed you were serious,

you would get it together someday.

I prayed for you instead of for my own strength.

Poem to My Pussy

I've violated you once again.

Putting trust in a man

That seemed to be different again.

I'm sorry, you didn't deserve this shit!

Trust will fuck you up.

It be having you out here thinking you lucked up.

Violating your first mind

And you saw all

the signs.

Same ol lines,

Roles,

Games.

That's been invented from the beginning of time.

Just keep your

Heart,

Head,

And your bed.

If you feel like sharing your bed temporarily,

that's ok, too.

Just protect your pearl

Because some men don't appreciate that either, boo.

I'm sorry, I haven't protected you.

Never Have I Ever

I've never witnessed

true, Black, love.

Where someone didn't have

to suffer.

Today, I choose me!

HATE

Why are we told not to hate?

It's a lot of shit I hate!

And a few people too!

It's just what it is!

Hate is an emotion that has roots deep,

and some of them have stewed in my mind

And festered in my heart.

Letter You Should've Found

Dear Dad,

How do you have an expectation

of how you want me to be?

You're trying to conduct the way I speak

And direct how I feel.

You want me to keep things real but if it's about you

I need to have an ounce of sympathy

and a gallon of compassion.

I need selective memory.

You want some type of control over me

because you're in your feels about everything

you did to me.

I love you,

but you cannot buy time back.

There are spaces you've missed

because you simply weren't there.

No, I'm not mad anymore.

Clearly.

Because my door was left open and

I let you dust your feet off and come right in.

I've listened to your tainted truths

that you try to pass off

as if I didn't watch you,

before I was 10

playing leapfrog and house with different women

while raising their children.

In and out of my life and C.J. Systems,

for reasons I don't know.

All I know is I grew up without you.

I'm another hurt woman on your list

because of your selfishness.

Don't Tell Me

Don't tell me what kind of woman I should be.

I wasn't put on this earth to comfort your insecurities.

Permission

Dear, me,

I give you permission to feel your way

through this place called life.

Like a river that flows endlessly,

speak your truth.

Breathe life into the creations

that have been brewing up in you.

Accept yourself.

Love yourself.

Be yourself.

Stay true to yourself.

#GirlDad

Why do daddies make their daughters feel hated?

Like we aren't the precious pearls

that come from their jewels?

No shade to Kobe's hashtag, #girldad.

All my life I dreamed of having a dad that was cool,

a dad that could pick me up when I was down,

make me laugh when I felt bad.

Instead, I'm another woman whose first love scar

came from her dad.

Although, my stepdads took steps and stepped in

to try to fill a void that you left empty,

nothing could ever fill it because

it was your spot to begin with.

My adolescence has passed and

I'm clocking 30.

So, now you wanna act like I'm Daddy's little princess?

And you get disappointed because you've found out,

from time to time,

I get treated like a man's mistress...

I laugh because maybe it's just karma

being returned to you.

P.S. I loved you, always!

You just showed up late to claim me.

I don't wanna be attached to your hashtag

because I know how it feels to think

you aren't loved by your dad.

Home

Home is where the heart is.

Or is my heart the place I made a comfortable place

that I call home?

Home is a place that I backtrack to

when I'm disoriented.

To get it right when I'm wrong.

There's no place like home.

At least, that's what Dorothy said.

A million restarts in my head.

Should I have gone this way or that way?

I should've said this or shouldn't have said anything.

Maybe things would be better

If I just wouldn't overthink

and remember the lessons from home.

Mama didn't raise a fool.

Although, I've done some foolish things

that might make you question my character.

Home is where the heart is.

When I lose my way, my internal porch light shines

to remind me to come back, to reset.

Learn from lessons,

and to never regret

the adventures that have given me experience.

Instead of a mind of curiosity

and close-minded spirit,

home is my safe space.

When I need a break from

everything that's going on in reality.

Home is a place where my heart

connects with my mind.

Home is the place I know that everything

is going to be all right.

Home is where the heart is.

My heart is free.

Tell 'Em I'm Blessed

Blessed, not stressed.

Positivity, not negativity.

Growth.

More permission

Dear me, I give you permission to feel

your way through this place called life.

Like a river that flows endlessly,

speak your truth.

Breathe life into the creations

that have been brewing up in you.

Accept yourself. Love yourself.

Be yourself.

Stay true to yourself.

Strong

Going through stuff alone

makes me feel like

I'm supposed to be tough.

Only because I'm left with no choice but to persevere

through tough and trying times!

I've been a

Black woman, strong,

Army strong,

the world's back bone,

for so long.

I've become nonimmune to disease.

My own flesh is attacking me.

First

I love me first!

For so long, I've been doing

shit in reverse.

For so long, my self esteem

was so low.

I allowed you to make me

a side-bitch.

I was blemished,

a hidden gem,

loving on people who placed me last,

until I woke up and smelled the coffee.

Now, that shit has come to an end.

And no mufucka,

I do not want to be friends!

Triumph and Trauma

Numb from trauma

passed down

from generation

to generation.

Reset from lessons

that's never changed.

Every book has remained the same,

until I spoke my truth.

Because those truths weren't mine,

they were ordered steps

that tried keeping my life in line.

And all that time,

I wasted time living a lie,

a life that wasn't mine.

I was destined to fly.

I was destined to soar.

I'm more than

a diploma,

a degree,

a 9 to 5.

It's natural that I've questioned myself,

and always wanted more.

More is embedded in my DNA.

And every day,

I strive to try to be better than the norm set

because I was born setting the tone.

My heart is free!

Good Woman

Lips as full as my breast,

hips wide as the Nile,

heart big as all outside;

her smile is grace.

GOD(DESS)

I wish I were a deity…

So that people would love and worship me

without even seeing me.

A face that can't be traced

but depicted everywhere

as if they've caught a glimpse

of my peace and beauty.

The tales about my beast, for some reason,

remain untold.

People don't pay attention to the wrath in me.

When I bring it, everyone blames my work

On some devil being

that they've never seen either.

I wish I were a deity.

But, if so, what kind would I be?

Would I be soft, merciful and full of grace

or would I be tough, combative,

and have the strength of a thousand rhinoceros?

Maybe I'd have the resilience of the stolen African?

Maybe if I were a deity, I'd be all those combined,

helping people balance out time.

And be sure to appear.

I'd be right on time like that other guy.

People would dance and sing songs for me.

People would love me and give in the name of me.

Love.

Wisdom.

NYC 2019

I'm a poet.

I'm a freedom fighter.

I'm a writer.

Click. Click.

I'm the lighter in the room

here to make your mind bloom.

Literary bombs in my mind,

ready to be detonated.

My stories are my journeys.

So, nope,

never outdated.

They're blueprints

and steps to show that I made it through.

And you can too!

Cosmic Girl

I came from

a cosmic being.

I mean look at me,

I'm a Queen!

I'm a Goddess!

I'm everything in between!

I'm a product of the moon and the sun.

Bronze skin and onyx twinkles for eyes.

I'm the past, present, and future.

Mean Mug

I keep one,

and naw you can't get a hug.

My number either, beat it!

Yea that's me

Living my life unapologetically.

Yea that's me,

Living as woman, Black and carefree.

Yea that's me,

loving my life and the things that come with it.

Yea that's me,

loving on me the way I'm supposed to be.

Yea that's me,

Free! I'm Free!

Yea, not caring what you think about me.

Yea,

I can't wait to actually be doing this shit.

Genie

They wanna rub on me like I'm genie

to grant their wishes like my name is Houdini.

They want that magic sauce.

They want the drip.

They want that Black girl clout,

cuz we the shit!

From different walks of life,

we are bold,

We are strong,

different and beautiful!

Every time you turn around there go another one

getting their bite on.

Wanna Christopher Columbus our style.

We are the originators,

while also staying ahead of the game to change it!

Trendsetters!

No one does it better!

Black woman,

I am you

and you are me!

Always duplicated but never replaced!

I don't care how much a counterfeit

is flaunted in your face.

No one will ever fill your place!

29

As I approach 30,

I realize,

I am the lock

and the key.

Manifesting what I want,

stepping into who I want to be.

Don't give a care who's hating on me.

The change I want will happen for me

because I said so.

My dreams are so vivid I can feel it,

bubbling over,

Careful, don't spill it.

New lines on these double lines.

The voice within me divine,

leaking proof.

Later *y'all* find out I'm telling the truth

because I'm walking in it.

I'm telling my truth.

Freeing myself.

Freeing my soul.

Freeing that girl that always wanted to be bold.

I am *Black Woman Magic*.

I am a *Goddess*.

I am the lock

and the key

ready to place all old shit behind me.

So I can live.

So that I can be

any and everything I was destined to be.

Whatever I went through,

didn't mold who I am.

Social Distance

I've been socially distancing

from the things that have been

dis-easing my spirit.

Disease (ing) my spirit!

It's hard because I love my friends.

I love my family.

But, loving you

doesn't stop the unintentional harm

that comes with you.

Sort of like all the disclosures

that come with pharmaceuticals...

I feel good temporarily,

but now I have more underlying issues.

With you.

With me.

With us.

So, I socially distance myself.

Mask up when you're around

because your attitude is contagious.

Your misery longs for company that I can't keep.

You need to feed off low vibrations like a parasite,

a leach,

Slowly sifting all the goodness from its host,

until you can claim another victim,

to sulk in a slumber that's hard to shake.

You're an anchor.

You're a weight.

I've been socially distancing

from the things that have been

dis-easing my spirit.

Socially distant because if I don't set the boundaries,

I'll be diseased by your spirit!

Mastered it

I'm free to be me and do whatever I please

because I define "MY" own destiny.

Everything that I desire, I will acquire!

All my praises I shout out to myself and the Most High.

I can officially say, "Mission complete,"

to "My" societal education

and continue to lay bricks,

a foundation for my future

and Generations.

I'm hooded.

Sankofa always moving forward

but never forgetting the path that brought me here.

2019 is my year.

Essmorra is Here!

Pussy Poem

My pussy be like warm apple pie.

You know, the kind

Niggas keep coming back for.

Would die to taste for.

My pussy be like a warm baptism,

have the whole congregation shouting.

My pussy be like Louisiana heat,

hot, sticky, and wet.

She so hot, leave *yo* ass out of breath.

My pussy be so marvelous.

She got niggas lying, saying they had her.

Got your imagination running wild.

for what you think this pussy might do.

My pussy be from Africa, the west coast, and the south.

My pussy has more value than diamonds in your mouth.

We don't need your money, we're already rich.

Plush.

Warm.

Pink.

My pussy will ruin your life if you don't treat her right.

My pussy is royalty.

Enough to make you want to prove your loyalty.

I thought you knew my pussy is golden.

A goddess.

I thought you knew who God is.

My pussy deserves a pedestal.

Queen of the jungle.

Call her, lioness.

My pussy be everything amazing you can imagine.

She brings light from her darkness.

My pussy be poised, siditty, and pretty.

But she be strong too.

My pussy can make you hum songs or

your ass be *sanging* the blues.

My pussy be the Alpha,

the Omega, and

the infinite quest to humanity.

My pussy be queen.

And she be king, too.

I thought y'all knew.

I thought y'all knew.

This pussy be birthing nations, too.

Put some respect on this pussy!

Kiss her and tell her thank you.

My pussy be powerful.

That WAP! (Wet Ass Pussy)

That nookie.

That cookie.

That gushy.

Mac and Cheese in a pot.

Tell her thank you

for those hard nights she kept you warm.

Forbidden Fruit

My hallways swelled

each time I inhaled and exhaled.

Another rush of my pussy nectar escaped,

opened the floodgates

as they entered Eden.

I showered her.

I showed her what heaven can really be like.

Fleshy bronzed gates,

pearls coated in chocolate.

Clits on lips.

Lips on tits.

A forbidden fantasy

that cums true.

And every now and then cum through.

Our temperature rises

like a humid Arkansas summer.

Hot,

humid,

and wet.

I love seeing those titties bouncing,

peeking from the land down under

wondering if we can cum.

The clock steadily ticking.

I'm waiting for her to explode.

She's waiting for me to explode.

In the forbidden land of tongues.

when she cums,

I cum.

We both cum,

in Eden.

Strong

When I think of a word

that signifies strength,

pussy comes to mind.

Pussy has birthed many moons

and many suns,

while pleasuring and pacifying

ungrateful Men.

Consensual or not.

Vibranium Pussy

I keep her veiled

because I've been told to keep her hidden.

If I give her up,

I'm told I'm sinning.

But,

I got *y'all* going out your way

to see the

true seventh wonder of the world,

my pussy.

Y'all out here

giving

currency,

diamonds,

gold,

your last.

You *wanna* see real power.

P.U.S.S.Y.

So, you do and say all the right things,

hoping

for a peek.

She remains a mystery,

the heart of my femininity.

Pulsating pineal love

and revolutionary grips got you

imagining the trips

she'll take you on.

Close your eyes.

Another set of lips,

too deep for two eyes to see.

You gotta close your eyes

to comprehend

this vibranium frequency

my pussy puts out.

Fantasizing

about my

two lips,

one pearl,

revolving around the world

since the beginning of

any life existence.

VIBRANIUM PUSSY!

VIBRANIUM PUSSY!

VIBRANIUM PUSSY!

Alkaline

Dripping,

like alkaline.

Before you enter

my portal,

ask yourself, are you aligned?

Are you ready for what comes with this ride?

Are you ready for what comes with me?

Are you ready to cum for me?

Are you truly ready to dive inside

this divine realm of true femininity?

And deliver?

Match my energy?

A whole new world

of infinite possibilities?

Exploring each other

and escaping illusions,

creating a real world,

where only you are included

and giving me your all.

Each and every bit.

No drop wasted,

I want all of that shit!

You hear me?

I said, I want it all!

I want to taste it.

So, strip down.

Naked.

Show me yourself,

from the crown of your head

to the souls of your feet.

Tell me again

what you said you'd do for me.

2020 Vision

I took some *L's* in 2020.

Some I didn't see coming.

But I still stand ten toes down, face forward,

because, backward isn't an option.

See, I can't complain much

because I'm here to write this poem.

Some stayed asleep, and yesterday was their last.

So, now lasting memories are all we have.

Every breath that we take, we all take for granted,

tippy toeing through infectious air,

like it ain't everywhere.

Walking around on eggshells,

just trying to make it through this pandemic

has fucked me up a lot

but made me see things a lot clearer.

It's easy to slip and wallow in your feelings,

but you have to gather yourself,

don't stop, get it, get it, push it to the limit,

Because this clock can't stop and won't stop,

so we gotta go and get it.

Strap up like you're about to deep-sea dive

under a warm sea, trying to get to pearls.

But protect yourself

from the bullshit out in this world.

Those *L's* don't define you,

only you do.

You're the author and illustrator of your own story.

Take it easy on yourself.

you're worthy and deserve some self-glory!

Beebo!

I've watched

you grow,

anticipating your

curly hair,

ten fingers and toes.

For 9 long months,

cooped up in your temporary room,

Nay Nay's womb.

Due in November,

your grand entrance coming soon!

Sleep

No more sleeping on myself.

I am everything and everything is me!

I am everything my

Mother, grandmother and great grand-mother

dreamed me to be.

I am the shit.

I am lit.

This *BLACK GIRL MAGIC* is deeply rooted within me!

Roots

Deep roots.

My tone is a warm brown.

Hair reaching for high power,

the trees resemble me,

I notice as I stand there with my bare feet

planted in the soil.

Giver of ALL life.

Strange people always wanting to touch,

admiring my strong exterior, hoping my majestic

leaves bless them.

Wondering how I've been able to stand

during the test of time.

Stages of many seasons,

from deep roots to strange fruit.

History duplicating itself.

Memoirs on repeat.

Nothing new under this sun,

same root, new leaves.

Resiliency elixir

fills the air,

Catching all of the carbon monoxide so,

you can breathe.

A new start.

Fresh air.

A do-over to right wrongs.

Rewriting and saving our history,

rebirthing the truth through new leaves.

Leaving lies behind us.

Washed-out lies don't define me (us).

Supremes

(Ode to the Black Woman)

We saved you,

fed you when you were eating cave food.

Birthed your nation

and ours, too.

From mammies to mommies,

legacies are born.

The ones you lynched,

burned and tried to bury with Jim Crow.

But,

we still grow

Because strength flows

through us effortlessly ....

Sprinkling black girl magic on you

since the beginning of time.

Breast feeding and nannying ingrates.

Nourishing your body, and you still

manage to find a way to hate.

There would be no you without me.

I think you need to rewind

And Readjust your history.

Don't question my experience.

Don't question my existence.

I deserve to

stand,

sit,

speak, and breathe

wherever I please.

A standing ovation,

fresh flowers at my feet.

I'm supreme.

I reign

for eternity.

Black Woman

Black woman,

I love you.

Black woman,

I appreciate you.

I thank goddess for you.

I give thanks to you.

For all your love that's unconditional

and the love that came with understood conditions

that's never been mentioned.

No one ever told you how much your heart

would ever have to bear.

You just did that shit,

because you care.

Bent.

Twisted.

Folded.

But, never contained to fit one mold.

Even when you're told how to be,

Black woman, you inspire me.

You inspire the world.

The universe lives between your thighs.

Orion's galaxy in your eyes,

foreseeing the next shift,

crowds tower around you

because you are the ultimate gift

to humanity.

Balancing out recurring turmoil with

love, patience, and forgiveness.

Black woman,

you are resilient.

The next time you need a reminder, look in the mirror.

Black woman,

you are brilliant.

It's the Truth

Careful, the truth can be deep.

So, it's what I speak.

Because I want it to seep down into your soul.

I want it to make you think.

I want it to leak like a serum

into your bloodstream.

Truth.

Can you handle the depths that it'll reach?

Can you handle what it'll make surface?

Truth, can face it?

Can you swallow it whole?

Can you take it?

There are levels to this shit.

It's beautiful and ugly at the same damn time.

War on Blaxxx

In a nation where *In God We Trust*,

but their God doesn't look like us.

Born in the belly of the beast,

but you get scared

when I unleash the beast in me.

You tell me not to act in rage

when we retaliate from your cowardly sins

against our sons and daughters.

Tired of y'all throwing the rock and hiding your hands.

Disguising racism in

police uniforms,

political suits,

army boots, and

sometimes even in classrooms.

You're provoked

by an unarmed Black body,

with their hands up,

on their knees?

If there's no hose to wash out your hate,

you use tear gas instead.

Protesters taking rubber bullets to their heads

because they're protesting against brutality

from the police.

You're provoked

by my skin because

here, *y'all* made me a sin.

You're afraid of Black love,

Black procreations.

Afraid because we have experience,

we've ruled all these nations,

survived on concrete plantations

and still shine.

Resilience is looking real scary to you, huh?

Our Ancestors are coming back

with a vengeance, might I add.

You may kill the plant

but the seeds are still rooted

like the popular trees that

bared strange fruit.

Fear doesn't live here

because it wasn't born here.

Neither does hate.

So, stop raking

your Black fears,

Black anger,

and

Black stereotypes

off onto my plate.

Conformity Won't Save You

(The price of resistance is great)

Closed minds trying to tell me how to feel.

They can't yet identify what's fake

or what's real.

Eager to make me fall in line with

their loud discomfort.

Left, right.,

Left, right.

Left, right.

Right, left.

Continuously marching to the beat in my chest,

and against the persuasion of conformity.

Because I know conformity will not save me.

So, I'm fighting with every ounce of resistance

against my blackness,

my Black womanhood,

against my *Hood*,

that's being bleached and washed clean

of all the positive imagery of people

who look like me.

From west coast to east coast,

midwest and deep in the south,

gentrification floods our streets.

But history is deeply rooted in me,

fighting to keep the fight of my people

resurrected in me.

Another One

Another

Black body slain.

Another

Black family's heart

filled with pain,

filled with Rage.

Another story where White people

with white privileges

and blood-stained hands

get to become the victors to tell fake news!

Pipeline

Cops for security?

Cradle to prison pipeline,

if you ask me.

Got these babies walking in single-file lines

On the right side of the hall

in a system that has blackballed

them before they've taken their first steps.

No books.

No tools.

No rules.

No guidance!

Just write-ups,

detention,

in-school and out-of-school suspension.

Lock them up, throw away the key.

Cradle to prison pipeline,

if you ask me.

Where is the chance for

our Black and Brown children?

Public schools are being policed

but nobody here polices the police!

Gentrification

Y'all gonna stop

trying to gentrify my plate,

gentrify my body,

gentrify my mind,

the air I breathe.

Telling me how to

walk,

talk,

trying to make me a token.

Speak

Goddess gave me permission to speak,

to talk my shit!

Sis, I'm allowed to flex,

express my stress.

Love.

Set the mood.

Chill mode or rude.

Heaven is

I sparked a tree and inhaled mother earths love.

When I exhaled her

she wrapped me tight and lifted me to the top

to admire how deep the sky is.

I used to think the ocean was deeper

as above so below right?

who taught us we couldn't have heaven on earth?

I've watched a Goddess part heaven

and give birth to her sun.

Heaven on earth is going round for round,

boxing that demon called depression.

My inner goddess forgiving me

when I fucked up a couple times.

But now I got the lesson.

To me that is heaven.

I count them mistakes, I mean blessings

them the guided steps from my ancestors to my own

path of righteousness

to self-love quests,

self-love,

self-care,

and just being aware

of my internal beauty and my ugly truths.

Who knew a goddess could be part beast too?

Shit.

Heaven is the best of both worlds.

Admiring my progress

from my throne.

Crown on swole

with manifestations falling to my feet.

I've conquered some levels of this game life.

I almost drowned in doubt.

Grabbed a pen and wrote until I seen my way out.

Gumbo

Fucking with an old soul twice removed

I was boiled in the stew

my ancestors brewed

Black ass love

back seat action

showered in

fucked around and find out

descendent of

cayenne attitudes

box braids with beads

better be in before

the streetlights come on

or *imma* get my ass beat

Timboots baggy jeans

and crop tops

I'm as majestic as my belly beads

or the cowries

my great great granny used to read

a sea of authenticity with a dash of Godfidence

because when I walk through the door

I know I got my Family tree up here with me

Imma whole mood

shit you would be too if you've had a teaspoon of what's

on my plate

God is good

Goddess is great

I'm a likeness of the two

beautiful like

pressured rice

when you get it right or

a diamond

like the ones Auntie Maya said were at the meeting of

my thighs

carrying on the writing torch because it's my birthright

to birth books

like Toni Morrison,

Audre Lorde and all the other greats.

I just *wanna* be great too!

About the Author

Essmorra a proud Alum of the University of Arkansas at Pine Bluff is from Oakland California byway of Pine Bluff, who now resides in Oklahoma City Oklahoma. As a performer of spoken word and writer of short stories, Essmorra desires is that her work is not only relatable but also uplifting. She wants the audience to know that they aren't alone.

Instagram @Essmorra

Email address: essmorra@gmail.com

Also by Essmorra:
"Who Hurt You, Sis?"

Now Available on Amazon